C000228100

STATIONS *of the*
Resurrection
from Easter to Pentecost

STATIONS *of the*
Resurrection
from Easter to Pentecost

Richard Q. Greatrex

Published by Redemptorist Publications
Wolf's Lane, Chawton, Hampshire, GU34 3HQ, UK
Tel. +44 (0)1420 88222, Fax. +44 (0)1420 88805
Email rp@rpbooks.co.uk, www.rpbooks.co.uk

A registered charity limited by guarantee
Registered in England 3261721

First published March 2019

Text by Richard Q. Greatrex
Edited by Caroline Hodgson
Designed by Eliana Thompson

ISBN 978-0-85231-545-3

Every effort has been made to trace copyright holders and to obtain their permission for the use of copyright material. The publisher apologises for any errors or omissions and would be grateful for notification of any corrections that should be incorporated in future reprints or editions of this book.

The publisher gratefully acknowledges permission to use the following copyright material:

Excerpts from the New Revised Standard Version of the Bible: Anglicised Edition, © 1989, 1995, Division of Christian Education of the National Council of the Churches of Christ in the United States of America. Used by permission. All rights reserved.

Printed and bound by Latimer Trend, Plymouth

Acknowledgements

These Stations of the Resurrection have grown through use with the worshipping community of Barrow Gurney and Flax Bourton and I am very thankful for their company on this journey.
I am also most grateful for the support, patience and expert eye of my wife, Mary-Jane, along with kind encouragement from the team at Redemptorist Publications.
That said, all errors are mine and mine alone – some might be irritating, others are, with hope, serendipitous.

Contents

Foreword by
Fr Denis McBride C.Ss.R.

Stations of the Resurrection

The longest story about Jesus in each of the four Gospels is the passion narrative which follows five great acts: the arrest of Jesus; the trial before the Jewish authorities; the trial before the Roman authority, the crucifixion and the death of Jesus; the burial of Jesus' body. That drama in five acts dominates the writing and the structure of each of the Gospels. It comes as no surprise, therefore, that for most Christians, probably the most distinct season of the Church's liturgical year is Lent when, for six weeks, we reflect on Jesus' journey to his appointment with death in the killing fields outside the walls of Jerusalem. That story of struggle and commitment in the face of gathering opposition is one which readily appeals to many people, not least because it can mirror something of their own journey. They can catch themselves on the Via Dolorosa, burdened under the weight of their own cross; and when they look over their shoulders they can see few people following in support.

The dominance of the passion narrative is reflected in the most enduring image of Jesus that has lasted through the ages: it is not Jesus the healer, or Jesus the teacher, or Jesus the risen Lord; it is Jesus at his most vulnerable on the cross. The crucifix has won out as the most enduring icon of Jesus, not least because who you believe Jesus to be depends on how you interpret his death.

It is the resurrection that truly interprets Jesus' death on the cross. This is expressed poetically in the ancient hymn that celebrates Christ Jesus:

> who, though he was in the form of God,
> did not regard equality with God
> as something to be exploited,
> but emptied himself,

1

taking the form of a slave,
being born in human likeness.
And being found in human form,
he humbled himself
and became obedient to the point of death –
even death on a cross.

Therefore God has highly exalted him
and gave him the name
that is above every name,
so that at the name of Jesus
every knee should bend,
in heaven and on earth and under the earth,
and every tongue should confess
that Jesus Christ is Lord,
to the glory of God the Father.   (Philippians 2:6-11)

What we celebrate in the resurrection is God's liberating love for his beloved Son. Resurrection is the Father's response to the cross, his defiant answer to a world that hoped violence could keep Jesus in its hold. In exalting Jesus, in raising him from the dead, God raised every value that Jesus ever treasured, every story that Jesus ever told, every preference that Jesus ever made, every purpose that Jesus ever followed. All this was given new life and new significance.

If death had spoken the final word about Jesus, it would only have been a matter of time before everything about Jesus would have been reduced to a curiosity, a forgettable footnote in the crowded history of lost causes. But God had the last word. As indeed God had the first.

The resurrection of Jesus was not a hysterical invention of people who refused to accept the death of their master. On the contrary, *resurrection is the original act of accepting Jesus' death*. The Father's act of raising Jesus from the dead is *the Father's way of accepting his Son's death*. Jesus is wakened to new life by the applause of his Father, by the sheer energy of his Father's love, by the loud shout of his Father's gratitude.

The dead Jesus has no alternative but to rise to the occasion. The tomb can never be his permanent address.

The good news is that the Father's affirmation is not confined to Jesus – it is extended to all who follow the way of the beloved Son. As Paul says: "When Christ who is your life is revealed, then you also will be revealed with him in glory." (Colossians 3:4) In the meantime, however, we struggle to let some of that glory shine through our halting efforts to follow the Lord. We know the way of the cross leads to our own doorstep and that we are challenged to take it. It leads us to the Father's ultimate affirmation, to the God who refuses to write an eternal R.I.P. over our resting place.

When I finished writing *Stations of the Cross: then and now*, I intended my next project to be *Stations of the Resurrection*. I cancelled that, without regret, when I read Richard Greatrex's manuscript which he submitted to Redemptorist Publications for a book of the same title. On reading his manuscript I saw that he had already accomplished beautifully what I was only dreaming about: he had written thoughtful and insightful reflections on the great journey from the closed tomb to Pentecost, accompanying them with appropriate scripture passages, prayers and some startling images that make you pause and wonder, and see anew. At first, I must confess, I was puzzled by some of his choices of artwork, but then I allowed them to speak with their own authority. I now appreciate how they offer their own elliptical and nuanced insight alongside the text.

Richard's writing and the images he has chosen to accompany each station work in tandem to lead us through the neglected cycle of the Church's year, from Easter to Pentecost. After the pilgrimage of Lent, many people might feel exhausted at the prospect of starting another one so soon. With Richard as our guide, however, this Easter pilgrimage is a very gradual and gentle journey; the pace is as leisurely as the insight is rewarding; it is an excursion of heart and mind that will surely deepen our faith in the risen Lord.

Denis McBride cssr **Denis McBride C.Ss.R.**

Introduction

A while ago we discovered in our garden a caterpillar belonging to a rare species of butterfly – a swallowtail – which really shouldn't have been found in our corner of England. It was sitting on a rock preparing to pupate. Forty days later there, on the same rock, rested the newly hatched adult, wings drying and unfurling in the autumn sunshine. Metamorphosis had taken place inside the dark cave of the pupal case, hatching had occurred in the early watches of the morning, and although we had missed all that, still our joy was immense. After a few hours, having been admired and photographed, the freshly born imago rose steadily on strong yellow and black wings shot through with an iridescence of blue and red. With surprising power for such a delicate creature it flew purposefully upwards over our village, and was gone.

Years later we still recollect that butterfly; its emergence was like a mini resurrection, a tiny jewelled reflection of the cosmos-changing events that we remember each Sunday at the Eucharist. Traditionally every Sunday is an Easter Day, a day of resurrection; but it is only Easter Day itself that opens the longest season in the Christian year, the Great Fifty Days that celebrate the immensity of Christ bursting from the tomb, breaking the chains of death, a festive time of great joy, hope and encouragement.

However, Easter Day is also the climax to the long Lenten season and Holy Week liturgies – momentous, moving and demanding, both physically and spiritually. It is hardly surprising, then, that by the end of the Triduum clergy and worshippers alike can feel so fatigued that it takes all their remaining reserves of strength to rekindle the light of Christ and sing it back into flame among an expectant Easter Day congregation. Then, just as Eastertide begins, ministry teams take off on recuperative holidays and congregational numbers tend to dip. While all highly understandable, this pattern cannot but detract from the immense and joyful impact of the resurrection and the life-imparting revolution it kick-starts.

The Stations of the Resurrection are a recently popularised devotional, spiritual and liturgical practice which is intended to refocus congregations on the grace and glory of Eastertide. Known also as the *Via Lucis*, or Way of Light, and introduced in the late 1980s, it provides a counterbalance to the centuries-old tradition of Stations (or Way) of the Cross - the *Via Crucis* - which draw us through Lent, into Holy Week, walking with Jesus to his destiny at Calvary. The Stations of the Resurrection send us from the doorway of the tomb out into a world transformed by Christ's victory over death. The one invites us to acknowledge the sacrifice and pain of discipleship; the other to experience the transfiguring commitment made at baptism to be agents of the resurrection in the world. Holy Saturday exists as the pivot between these two forms of devotion, attached on one side to the events of Good Friday and on the other to those of Easter Day: imagine it as the centre of a spinning propeller - seemingly still while all around is turbulence and violent activity. It is the moment, like a full point at the end of a sentence, that stops us dead, gives us room to reflect, choose to halt or move on.

Since their inception in the fourteenth century, the Stations of the Cross have continued to evolve and develop. Initially varying significantly in number from between five and thirty-six, stations were eventually fixed at fourteen in 1731 by Pope Clement XIII. Of these, nine were biblically based and five inspired by popular legends and stories. In recent years fourteen scriptural stations have become far more widespread, with a fifteenth, the resurrection, often serving as a postscript to the set. Many welcome this biblical focus on the fourteen images, but the fifteenth is more problematic: including it during Lent, and especially Holy Week, shifts our focus in anticipating the resurrection before the full impact of the crucifixion, perhaps even our part in it, has been assimilated. Furthermore, it almost treats the resurrection as an "add-on", compressing all its complexity, intricacy and immeasurable importance down into one single image.

This is where the Stations of the Resurrection prove their value, allowing space for the resurrection to breathe and shine with many facets. Still emerging from infancy, their precise contents are yet to be tightly defined: many churches and individuals are currently in the process of exploring different numbers of stations and combinations of images. Some begin in the darkness of the sealed tomb; others with the flashlight of resurrection itself. Some will run through forty days ending at Ascension Day; others traverse the Great Fifty Days of the Lukan resurrection narrative, concluding at Pentecost by sending us out into the world as the newly formed Church, whose very existence is living in and driven by the light of that resurrection. The Church of England, in its official *Common Worship* seasonal resource book, *Times and Seasons*, goes even further, offering nineteen stations that end post-Pentecost with the conversion of Saul.

In contrast to the mixed ingredients for the traditional Stations of the Cross, the focus for the Stations of the Resurrection has been exclusively scriptural from the outset. Each station demonstrates the profound impact of Christ's resurrection appearances on the disciples, beginning with Mary Magdalene, illuminating how Jesus' first followers are transformed from faltering, fearful remnants of a failed faction, locked away from the world, into bold proclaimers of the Gospel. Along the way there is much heart-searching and healing, revelation and doubt, truth-telling and story-gathering, unfolding of scripture and the opening of minds to the unending possibilities of God's love.

The Stations of the Resurrection are one way to reinvigorate our flagging physical, emotional and spiritual energies in Eastertide by aiming to sustain throughout the whole season that sense of wonder and celebration we strive to evoke in our Easter Day liturgies. They also provide an opportunity to explore how, in the light of the resurrection and through their encounters with the risen Christ, the disciples grew from a broken rabble to determined and visionary founders of the Church. In the joy of Easter lies our confidence as Christ's hands and feet in the world: sometimes, in an environment of falling church commitment and competing or positively hostile tides of secular values, we need to be reminded of where our strength lies, that we are an Easter people and that Alleluia! is our song.

It is my hope that the prayers and reflections contained here might be a starting point for your own individual or communal exploration of the resurrection in your life or your community. The accompanying devotions have been used over several years within the parishes I serve and are offered with the love and prayers of a small rural community where we still look for the miracle swallowtails among the everyday flutter of cabbage white butterflies.

The Flax Bourton Swallowtail,
Richard Greatrex,
acrylic and gold leaf on wood, 2015

How to use this book

This book has been designed for both public and private devotion. One option for private use would be to pray through the whole book in one sitting, or you may like to include the readings, reflections and prayer as part of your daily rhythm of personal devotion, especially during Eastertide.

Some people may find it helpful to write down their response to each station – asking questions about what happened next, how those involved might have felt, thought or acted, how they react emotionally to the events described, what difference it might make for their lives. The Stations of the Resurrection, like the Stations of the Cross, are intended for use with pictorial images. The selection included in this book aims to offer fresh insight into well-known biblical passages, to "tell it slant", in Emily Dickinson's words. However, if you don't find these illustrations work for you, then take a long pause, close your eyes and imagine each scene as vividly as possible; or, if you can, draw or paint your response to each event, perhaps even including yourself in each picture.

Both Stations of the Cross and Stations of the Resurrection are filled with imagery exploring journeying and are perfect for forms of public devotion that make use of a whole building, or grounds. I have encountered stations produced for PowerPoint presentation, which is sensible in a small space or for a congregation with mobility issues, but they work best as an active pilgrimage. If you wish to obtain commercially available posters to place around your worship space, care will be needed to ensure a good match between image and reflection.[1] As a church community you may be inspired to devise your own paintings, banners or collages to accompany the devotions here, or more simply to create a physical set of stations, constructed using readily obtainable objects, ideas for which are outlined in detail at the end of the book.

---

1   McCrimmons' *Way of Light* (www.mccrimmons.com/shop/stations-of-the-resurrection) offers sixteen images that correspond accurately with these reflections.

When setting out the stations around your building it is worth considering certain key factors. If you are in a church that already contains a set of Stations of the Cross, you will need to decide how the Stations of the Resurrection relate to them. The number will be different for a start, so it might be best to create a fresh trail, using different aspects of the building – pillars and pew ends – while also maximising ease of accessibility for participants to move around and view each image.

My preference is to start with Station 1: The Sealed Tomb on an outside door, with everyone gathered, if possible, in the church porch. At the end of the station the door, like the stone covering the tomb, is opened – a physical reminder of the changed perspective that resurrection brings. I also like to place the final station, 16: Pentecost, on the inside of the same door, which I open at the end of the reflection, bringing the congregation back into contact with the wider world and sending us out, like the disciples, to share the good news of the resurrection.

This book contains all the necessary material for the leader of the devotions, but it makes sense for the opening and closing prayers, together with the responses at each station, to be typed up into a congregational booklet. Singing is often a significant ingredient of pilgrimage; as yet, however, there is no equivalent to the *Stabat Mater* for Stations of the Resurrection. A selection of potentially suitable hymns is listed towards the end of the book, but you may also have some Eastertide favourites. It may be wise to incorporate these into the congregational booklet for ease of use. Above all, you will want to remember that these are Eastertide devotions, full of the joy and wonder of resurrection. Alleluia!, therefore, is an appropriate response to be used fulsomely.

Prayers at the start of the service

Opening response, reading and prayer

In the name of the Father, and of the Son, and of the Holy Spirit.
Amen.

Alleluia. Christ is risen.
He is risen indeed. Alleluia.

> For if we have been united with him in a death like his, we will certainly be united with him in a resurrection like his… But if we have died with Christ, we believe that we will also live with him… So you also must consider yourselves dead to sin and alive to God in Christ Jesus.
>
> Romans 6:5. 8. 11

We say together:
Risen Lord,
As we set out on this pilgrimage of faith,
we pray that you will guide our steps
so that we may find you in both darkness and light.
Here we stand among Mary Magdalene, Peter, John
and all the disciples
as witnesses of your triumph over sin and death.
Direct our meditations
that the seeds of your resurrection
eastering in our hearts
may take root, blossom and be fruitful
in our lives.
Amen.

THE FIRST STATION

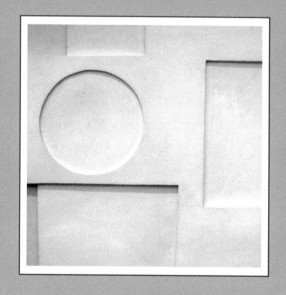

The Sealed Tomb

1934 (Relief), **Ben Nicholson, 1934**

Circle and square side by side, white on white, defined by shadow. The square, the tomb, expands, made limitless by our unfocused fears. Perhaps the circle, the stone, is too small to seal it, but without it the tomb would be incomplete.

Opening response

Jesus said: "I am the resurrection and the life."
Lord, you are our way, our truth and our life. Alleluia.

Reading

Matthew 27:57-66

When it was evening, there came a rich man from Arimathea, named Joseph, who was also a disciple of Jesus. He went to Pilate and asked for the body of Jesus; then Pilate ordered it to be given to him. So Joseph took the body and wrapped it in a clean linen cloth and laid it in his own new tomb, which he had hewn in the rock. He then rolled a great stone to the door of the tomb and went away. Mary Magdalene and the other Mary were there, sitting opposite the tomb.

The next day, that is, after the day of Preparation, the chief priests and the Pharisees gathered before Pilate and said, "Sir, we remember what that impostor said while he was still alive, 'After three days I will rise again.' Therefore command that the tomb be made secure until the third day; otherwise his disciples may go and steal him away, and tell the people, 'He has been raised from the dead', and the last deception would be worse than the first." Pilate said to them, "You have a guard of soldiers; go, make it as secure as you can." So they went with the guard and made the tomb secure by sealing the stone.

Reflection

Like a full stop carved out of limestone, a great boulder is cast in front of the entrance of the tomb. The story ends here; it is the point of no return. We have reached the bottom of the contract and there is no small print, no get-out clause. It is an impenetrable cataract rolling across a pupil, sealing it so that no sliver of the light of the world can slip out, sneak past the guards, break into the darkness and dance with the shadows.

Joseph has been busy – it is all he can do: organise, problem-solve, make the best of a bad situation, throw money at it. But he is broken, his secret hopes buried. Even so, it is a bold gesture, giving dignity to the corpse of a "criminal", rescuing it from the fate of some refuse pit and laying it in his own expensively procured grave. More than that, he is declaring his hand, openly backing the losing side in a political power struggle, a battle for the soul of the people. His respectable status has just taken a massive hit.

Mary Magdalene and the other Mary will busy themselves with the task of cleaning the body, packing linen wraps with preserving and sweet-smelling herbs. But that can't be done today. Distraught and confused, they need to turn to something practical and tangible; stillness is unbearable – their minds have too much to process. Dusk has now fallen and it feels as if dawn can never return.

The Pharisees too have been on the go – planning, plotting, twisting this way and that in the glare of Roman attention, trying to defend their patch, preserve the integrity of their religion and the last shreds of their authority. The deed has been done, the problem neutralised; yet they are still on edge, needing to bury this story once and for all.

One question resurfaces again and again: "Where is God in all this?" There is an answer behind that limestone door, lying passive, limp-limbed on the cooling boards. It is an answer that gives no reprieve, generates a barracking swarm of further questions and feels as small, dark, unfathomable as a firmly inked full point.

When all hope has been buried, where do we go from here?

Prayer

Lord Jesus, Author of all, Word made flesh,

you wrote life's story, then you entered the pages,

to break open the boundaries that hold us back from your love.

Lord of life, walled up in a cold, dark tomb,

be with all those who suffer in secret,

whose pain is hidden from the world's gaze.

Bring peace to their hearts and the light of justice to their cause.

Amen.

Closing response

We praise you, O Lord, and we bless you:

**By your dying, death was destroyed,
by your rising, life was renewed,
by your Spirit, may we be filled with your glory.**

THE SECOND
STATION

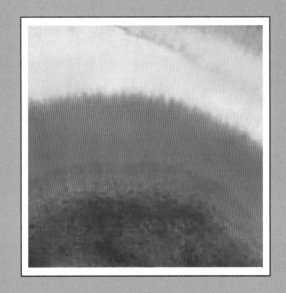

The Resurrection

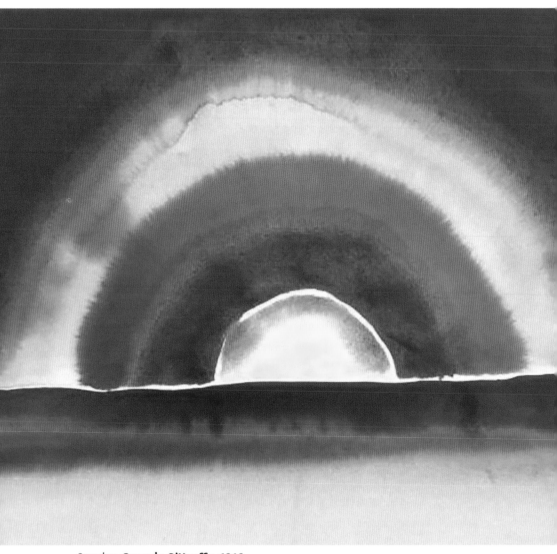

Sunrise, **Georgia O'Keeffe**, 1916

The sun rises as a seed germinating, pushing upwards, out from the fertile darkness of the earth.

Opening response

Jesus said: "I am the resurrection and the life."
Lord, you are our way, our truth and our life. Alleluia.

Reading

1 Corinthians 15:20-22

But in fact Christ has been raised from the dead, the first fruits of those who have died. For since death came through a human being, the resurrection of the dead has also come through a human being; for as all die in Adam, so all will be made alive in Christ.

Reflection

"Now the green blade riseth from the buried grain."[2] Re-examine that boulder, that full stop. You could say it resembles a giant seed, hard-cased, dead-looking, unprepossessing; a symbol of stubbornness, patience, potential. Was the resurrection inevitable? Perhaps this is what the Pharisees feared. Their solution? A massive door, sealed so no breath could slip by, armed guards to keep the curious, mischievous or determined at bay, and lies about a stolen corpse.

When Jesus died the veil of the Temple was torn in two, the partition between humanity and divinity was ripped apart. When Jesus was born he broke through the fleshly barrier of the womb. The Word pitching his tent among us – the nomadic God of Moses, whose lodging was the peripatetic Ark of the Covenant – was making footprints on the sand. The Temple had outlived its purpose; and now these new walls loomed impenetrably – smaller, tighter, far more claustrophobic – no decoration of gold-winged cherubim here; no fragrance of the incense of sacrifice. Solomon wondered as he dedicated the first Temple: "Will God indeed dwell on the earth? Even heaven and the highest heaven cannot contain you, much less this house that I have built!" (1 Kings 8:27). Up until his death Jesus' disciples had been slowly, falteringly, reaching the conclusion that God was truly inhabiting the earth. Now the tomb was going to bear witness that God could not, cannot, be contained.

Buried grain needs time in the dark before it splits open and new life emerges. When Egyptian tombs have been broken into, two thousand-year-old seed has proved viable. As the green blade rises, so from the cool depths of the grave Christ does what Christ, what God, was destined to do: Christ himself rises. The nature of God is to love creation; God in Christ cannot be separated from the beloved. Love will come again. There is no trumpet, no torn veil, no guiding star, no heavenly choir, no adoring shepherds, no lowing beasts. Resurrection aestivates to germinate among shadows, un-witnessed, un-regarded.

2 "Now the Green Blade Riseth", by John Macleod Campbell Crumo.

Prayer

Living Lord,

when your resurrection seeded in the dark,

you raised not only yourself but us,

to be new people, fashioned in your own image,

seeds sent out over the earth to spread your good news.

Help us to be that good news,

even when we feel smothered by care and strife,

so that we might share with everyone we meet the life your grace brings.

Amen.

Closing response

We praise you, O Lord, and we bless you:

**By your dying, death was destroyed,
by your rising, life was renewed,
by your Spirit, may we be filled with your glory.**

THE THIRD STATION

They Found the Stone Rolled Away

Scorpio Series 3, No. 9, **Wilhelmina Barns-Graham, 1997**

The dis-arrangement of line and form achieves a harmonious whole – the orange circle, like the stone of the tomb, is being pushed away. The teetering blue, red and white uprights are, like the women, disconcerted by the circle/stone's disarray, or like falling dominoes, their arrival is one in a chain of causes that precipitates an inevitable destiny.

Opening response

Jesus said: "I am the resurrection and the life."
Lord, you are our way, our truth and our life. Alleluia.

Reading

Luke 24:2-3

They found the stone rolled away from the tomb, but when they went in, they did not find the body.

Reflection

"Laid in the earth like grain that sleeps unseen: Love is come again, like wheat that springeth green."[3] His death had been public, witnessed by many. The evidence that his life had departed was laid out for all to see. Hung on a cross, a spear in the side, Jesus was no more. For his friends and followers to believe anything else would mean scaling immense barriers and holding firmly to an untested hope – resurrection. His burial was in secret, in the dark, known by few, attended by only the bravest and most indomitable. The stone that blocked the entrance tight was as huge and heavy as all the black thoughts and memories that were crushing out of mind the words of Jesus – his prophecies, repeated over and again to dim ears: that the Son of Man must go to Jerusalem, suffer, die and on the third day rise again. If that Temple curtain, torn in two at Jesus' death, marked the sundering of the borders between heaven and earth, then this stone, in all its rearing solidity, was a last-ditch attempt to close down the blazing potential of divine reconciliation with creation.

But as the new dawn fades, love comes again. Just as bluebells grow back every year, pushing their way through tarmac and concrete, so hope springs green. Tons of limestone were shifting, the entrance was unguarded, the sweet air of day swirled inside the tomb. A transformation in the very fabric of existence was taking place, in the dark, in the shadows, in the quiet of night. Distraught hearts and minds were still exhaustedly racing to process the vicious destruction of the light-filled future they had sold everything to follow. How could they come to understand, accept, celebrate that the world they had woken up to was turning on a different plane?

---

3   "Now the Green Blade Riseth", by John Macleod Campbell Crum.

Prayer

Almighty God,

your strong arm delivers,

you sweep the powerful from their thrones

and raise up the weak.

May your strength prevail when we feel too drained

to roll away the stones that block our pathway.

And may we use what strength you offer us,

to give heart to those whose voices go unheeded:

whenever there seems to be nothing left,

may the resurrection of your beloved Son

sustain and unite us in your compassionate love.

Amen.

Closing response

We praise you, O Lord, and we bless you:

**By your dying, death was destroyed,
by your rising, life was renewed,
by your Spirit, may we be filled with your glory.**

THE FOURTH STATION

The Women
at the Tomb

The Three Marys at the Tomb, **Lorenzo Monaco, 1396**

An explosion of colour, a riot of fecundity curling, unfurling out of the page – yet there is order and balance. As the women meet the possibility of the resurrection, so they stand close to the fulcrum on which the restored creation pivots.

Opening response

Jesus said: "I am the resurrection and the life."

Lord, you are our way, our truth and our life. Alleluia.

Reading

Luke 24:4b-5

Suddenly two men in dazzling clothes stood beside them. The women were terrified and bowed their faces to the ground, but the men said to them, "Why do you look for the living among the dead? He is not here, but has risen."

Reflection

The entrance is unguarded, the stone cast aside. The grave clothes are abandoned and the tomb is empty, empty apart from the women's own whispered and echoing voices. Frightened voices – where is the body? What have they done to him? Excited voices – what does this mean? Do you remember what he said would happen to him? Sceptical voices – what sort of a trick is this?

Then suddenly two figures in dazzling clothes are standing beside them. Is this a trap? Have they blocked the entrance? Are the women now the ones entombed? Are they to be counted as dead? They wrestle with their senses, which are assaulted from all directions. Take sight – they have seen the stone rolled away, the body absent, the iridescent angel clothes. Take smell – there is no stench of death, the tomb is fresh and airy. Take touch – they had felt the weight and solidity of the stone and had handled the grave clothes which were folded neatly as if by someone with no need to hurry, with time to spare. Take taste – the tang of fear in their mouths. Now they hear: "Why do you look for the living among the dead? He is not here, but has risen."

The breath has been knocked clean out of them. After the vicious spectacle of his crucifixion everything that mattered had been destroyed; the women had felt utterly stricken, all hope and purpose torn from them. But now, where was this tumult of emotions leading them? Was there hope after all? Could they trust the evidence of their senses? Could they truly believe what their Lord had said about his death and rising again?

Prayer

Risen Lord Jesus,

when you broke free of the tomb

you overturned rules and systems that chain us to false expectations.

Just as your friends and followers needed the presence of angels

to prompt them to grasp the possibilities of your resurrection,

we ask you to equip us to be your messengers,

overcoming fear and allowing others to see your infinite love

working throughout the twists and turns of life.

Amen.

Closing response

We praise you, O Lord, and we bless you:

**By your dying, death was destroyed,
by your rising, life was renewed,
by your Spirit, may we be filled with your glory.**

THE FIFTH STATION

The Women
Meet the
Risen Lord

Arlésiennes (Mistral), **Paul Gauguin, 1888**

Wrapped up tight, hands over faces, the front two women seem unable to allow what they are seeing to break into their comprehension. Their guard is up, they don't want to be called to expect the unexpected. Rather, they long to deal with their grief through the orderliness of ritual.

Opening response

Jesus said: "I am the resurrection and the life."
Lord, you are our way, our truth and our life. Alleluia.

Reading

Matthew 28:8-10

So they left the tomb quickly with fear and great joy, and ran to tell his disciples. Suddenly Jesus met them and said, "Greetings!" And they came to him, took hold of his feet, and worshipped him. Then Jesus said to them, "Do not be afraid; go and tell my brothers to go to Galilee; there they will see me."

Reflection

Belief has taken hold, hope is rising; and yet the powers of this world are strong, conspiracies are many and serpentine. The possibility that this is a cruel trick persists in their minds. Worse still would be an arrest by the authorities before they had a chance to tell the rest of Jesus' followers. Then the potential offered by the resurrection would be stillborn, buried grain that germinates but never reaches the surface to see the light of day.

All of a sudden Jesus is here: he is before them on the path. The garden is in blossom, the sun has risen, night has been banished. Their turmoil dissolves into overwhelming joy as they intuitively bow down to worship their Lord. Surely this could not be a longed-for apparition of their own making? Reaching out instinctively to touch him, they cannot help but question whether these are the feet whose scars from endless journeys they have tended, soothed and anointed. They had washed those feet many times over the years, a kindness offered whenever he arrived back at camp after a hard day travelling the villages, walking dusty and stony roads. The lines on his soles tell a story they each know well – they are proof that cannot lie. They take hold of his feet and in cradling the familiar they also find new scars, deeper wounds that sing out with the ferocious pain of his most recent journey.

But now, he tells them, the time for fear is over and it is their turn to travel – "Go, tell my disciples to meet me in Galilee".

Prayer

Living Son of the loving God,

the women who had the courage to visit your tomb

were greeted by your consoling words, "Do not be afraid."

We pray for women all around the world

who are hard-pressed, ill-treated, disenfranchised;

that through your resurrection their fears may turn to hope

and that they may find the strength, skills and tools

to live life in all its fullness.

Amen.

Closing response

We praise you, O Lord, and we bless you:

**By your dying, death was destroyed,
by your rising, life was renewed,
by your Spirit, may we be filled with your glory.**

THE SIXTH STATION

Peter and John
Run to the Tomb

Riace Figures, **Elisabeth Frink, 1987-1989**

Peter and John, two aspects of Everyman, race to the tomb. Naked, unguarded, stripped down to their elemental nature by their grief, perhaps they are desperate to catch hold of any sign of hope.

Opening response

Jesus said: "I am the resurrection and the life."
Lord, you are our way, our truth and our life. Alleluia.

Reading

John 20:3-10

Then Peter and the other disciple set out and went towards the tomb. The two were running together, but the other disciple outran Peter and reached the tomb first. He bent down to look in and saw the linen wrappings lying there, but he did not go in. Then Simon Peter came, following him, and went into the tomb. He saw the linen wrappings lying there, and the cloth that had been on Jesus' head, not lying with the linen wrappings but rolled up in a place by itself. Then the other disciple, who reached the tomb first, also went in, and he saw and believed; for as yet they did not understand the scripture, that he must rise from the dead. Then the disciples returned to their homes.

Reflection

Peter, man of action and authority, leader of those who remain, and John, meditator, dreamer and revealer of visions. They have heard the stories – breathless chatter, urgent, nonsensical gobbets of mysterious tales, hopeful yet confused: guards deserted, stone removed, body gone, grave clothes folded, strange messengers with stranger words and then Jesus, talking, commanding. And they recognised him by the shape of his feet!

Whatever has happened it has turned their despair into fearsome hope – hope filled with many questions, but still hope where a few hours ago there was none. Their faces are changed, filled with a new light. Peter and John, in their different ways, come to one conclusion: they must see this for themselves. They start out together, a walk turning to a run. Perhaps fisherman Peter is carrying more weight, or perhaps John's desire is more urgent. He gets there first. Even so, his longing doesn't take him over the threshold. Does he need to evaluate each part of what he is experiencing before he takes the next step? He sees the guards gone, the stone standing aside, a gaping entrance beckoning him in. He peers inside, sees the absence of the expected, the space where the body should be, and he holds back. The implications need to be thought through; the message God is giving needs praying through. For John, standing on the edge of possibility is in itself a valid and vital place to be.

Peter, meanwhile, breathlessly arrives at the threshold. His impetuosity pushes him over and into the tomb. He observes all the discarded accoutrements of burial, with the head cloth rolled up separately. Does he take in the details, or just the general impression? For him this is the genesis of a story that needs chasing down – but at this stage he doesn't have the evidence, or the faith, to commit to a conclusion.

Now that Peter has passed through the doorway, crossed the liminal space, broken the stasis, filled the emptiness with his agitated aliveness, John takes his first steps over the threshold. He sees the same details; but for John the space releases unfathomable height and breadth and depth: the evidence has shifted his faith into a new dimension. He sees and believes – the Lord is risen, he is risen indeed.

Prayer

Heavenly Father,

in your wisdom you create every person as an individual,

each in a unique relationship with the world.

We thank you that, just like Peter and John,

each one of us has our own way of approaching, examining,

evaluating, trusting and believing.

May opportunities to meet you open up to everyone,

whether in times of emptiness or fullness,

that the breath of resurrection might bring fresh vitality to our lives.

Amen.

Closing response

We praise you, O Lord, and we bless you:

By your dying, death was destroyed,
by your rising, life was renewed,
by your Spirit, may we be filled with your glory.

THE SEVENTH STATION

Angels at the
Empty Tomb

Mary Magdalene Questions the Angels in the Tomb, **James Tissot, 1886–1894**

The doorway constrains Mary, pushes her limbs out at awkward angles – in contrast to the sublime synchronicity of the angels. Will she be able to move into the same sacred space as the angels and grasp the universe-shaking vastness of their message?

Opening response

Jesus said: "I am the resurrection and the life."
Lord, you are our way, our truth and our life. Alleluia.

Reading

John 20:11-13

But Mary stood weeping outside the tomb. As she wept, she bent over to look into the tomb; and she saw two angels in white, sitting where the body of Jesus had been lying, one at the head and the other at the feet. They said to her, "Woman, why are you weeping?" She said to them, "They have taken away my Lord, and I do not know where they have laid him."

Reflection

Here is a woman whose life had been transformed by an itinerant preacher from Galilee. At a word from his lips, a touch from his fingers, all the horrors of her past, a sevenfold torment of pain, disgust, terror, nightmares, self-loathing, fear, anger – were cast out into nothingness, torn from her heart, her mind, her soul, overwhelmed by grace. She was born anew. Daylight flooded into the darkest corners of her world. She gave up all that she had to embrace a new way of living, travelling, like the Ark of the Covenant, in a nomadic caravan across the land. She became a disciple, a follower of the preacher, seeing life anew through his words, his thoughts, his visions of infinite love.

And then slicing into her newfound joy was the claggy, cloying, musclebound hatred of the system, of the rule-makers who enforced their laws with whip and spear. Her Lord, her teacher, her Saviour, was torn away from her, from all of them. His end was swift, bitter and bloody, a national disgrace, hung out for the public to see his ignominy. She could feel those demons of old gnawing at the edges of her mind, clawing towards her heart.

"Woman, why are you weeping?" Why would she not be weeping? Everything that mattered to her, everything that gave her hope in the future, dignity in her womanhood, belief in humanity, had been ripped to shreds, hung on a cross and left out in the sun to die. Then, just when there seemed to be some possibility of a respectful rest for his body, in a freshly made tomb, which she could visit and where she could mourn fully and learn to, in professional speak, "come to terms with her loss", even that kindness was murdered and his body gone.

What use were angels when the whole point of her life had been stolen, so that not even his scent remained? What hope was there for her now? What hope was there for any of his followers? Would there ever again be any good news to tell the world?

Prayer

Saviour God,

sometimes we feel so weighed down

that all help seems to be no help at all.

During these times may we discern your voice

and remember that you never let us go.

We pray for all who mourn,

that out of their sadness may come a new understanding:

that each and every one of us

is bound together eternally by your love.

Amen.

Closing response

We praise you, O Lord, and we bless you:

**By your dying, death was destroyed,
by your rising, life was renewed,
by your Spirit, may we be filled with your glory.**

THE EIGHTH STATION

Mary Magdalene
Meets the
Risen Lord

Garden in Shoreham, **Samuel Palmer, c. 1830**

With Samuel Palmer every landscape or vista, no matter how domestic or
parochial, is invested with visionary, divine potentiality. Here a garden,
redolent with spring blossom, could easily be the site of Mary's meeting with
the divine gardener.

Opening response

Jesus said: "I am the resurrection and the life."
Lord, you are our way, our truth and our life. Alleluia.

Reading

John 20:14b-18

She turned round and saw Jesus standing there, but she did not know that it was Jesus. Jesus said to her, "Woman, why are you weeping? For whom are you looking?" Supposing him to be the gardener, she said to him, "Sir, if you have carried him away, tell me where you have laid him, and I will take him away." Jesus said to her, "Mary!" She turned and said to him in Hebrew, "Rabbouni!" (which means Teacher). Jesus said to her, "Do not hold on to me, because I have not yet ascended to the Father. But go to my brothers and say to them, 'I am ascending to my Father and your Father, to my God and your God.'" Mary Magdalene went and announced to the disciples, "I have seen the Lord"; and she told them that he had said these things to her.

Reflection

"Woman, why are you weeping?" That question again. How can she reply? Any truthful answer would reveal too much of herself; it would be too complicated. Instead she responds with her own question.

"Tell me where you have laid him." The physical presence of his body is something she desperately needs. It is something she understands, a tangible link back to her memories, his preaching, teaching, healing, all the possibilities he offered. Take away his body and the focus for grief will disappear. It will become even harder for her and the other disciples to remember him well and to remember him collectively. As a group they will lose heart, fracture, disperse, find his vision blurring to incomprehensibility, like a sandstorm blown against glass.

"Mary!" A single word – her own identity – the one he called her back to when he drew her out of illness and into the wondrous beauty of new life. "Mary!" Calling her again, pulling her upwards out of grief into the fresh light of a new dawn. She needs nothing else to believe. And then she realises she does: she needs to hold him, to be anchored by the reality of his physicality. He is back, her teacher, her Lord, the one who redeems life for ever.

Jesus, however, knows that her belief is stronger than that. She is stronger than that, and maybe than the rest of his followers as well. She may not yet understand it, but her acceptance of the reality of his resurrection presence does not depend upon the physical body she had been so desperate to find. So he tells her, "Do not hold on to me." The negative is prelude to a positive: "Go, tell my brothers that you have seen me and that I am with our Father, our God." Mary Magdalene, the disciple to the disciples: she is the one entrusted with the message. Through her tears the seed is germinated that will become the Church.

Prayer

Living Word,

you called us by name and we are yours.

When you spoke Mary's name

you gave her back her identity, her strength, her vision.

Forgive us for all the times

we have not treated other people as children of God,

when we have been disrespectful, disdainful or distant,

when we have allowed anonymity to colour our behaviour.

By your grace may we turn again to strive to be your community,

where the worth of each individual is acknowledged and celebrated.

Amen.

Closing response

We praise you, O Lord, and we bless you:

**By your dying, death was destroyed,
by your rising, life was renewed,
by your Spirit, may we be filled with your glory.**

THE NINTH STATION

The Walk
to Emmaus

The Mule Track, **Paul Nash, 1918**

The Emmaus road may have been the path home, but it meant crossing occupied territory. In their minds the disciples were in No Man's Land – their man, the second Adam, Christ, was dead. How could their faith survive this devastation? The women insisted that Jesus is risen – was that a credible hope or another crater for them to fall into?

Opening response

Jesus said: "I am the resurrection and the life."
Lord, you are our way, our truth and our life. Alleluia.

Reading

Luke 24:15-16. 25-27

While they were talking and discussing, Jesus himself came near and went with them, but their eyes were kept from recognising him… Then he said to them, "Oh, how foolish you are, and how slow of heart to believe all that the prophets have declared! Was it not necessary that the Messiah should suffer these things and then enter into his glory?" Then beginning with Moses and all the prophets, he interpreted to them the things about himself in all the scriptures.

Reflection

From Jerusalem to Emmaus was a full day's journey if you were fit, well-provisioned and motivated. It crossed a range of terrain, some rocky, some semi-desert. Was this trip a good idea? They had to escape from the claustrophobia of the upper room, however, where all the followers were gathered together, obsessing, worrying, ruminating over and over everything that had happened, spinning it in a thousand different directions, jumping with fright every time the door rattled, or the wind smacked at the shutters, terrified that soldiers were about to storm in. It was bad enough when Jesus had just been killed, but now, with all these stories whirling around from the women about angels and the empty tomb, and Peter's confusion when he returned breathless from the garden, and John's certainty, it was all too much to take. Decision made, they risked detection by the milling city soldiers and got out.

They needed a breather, to go home to Emmaus for a few days, take stock and gain perspective. It wasn't as refreshing a walk as they were hoping for, though; the knowledge that Jesus was dead seemed to have leached all the green out of the countryside, turned the landscape hostile. At the back of their minds were so many thorny issues they felt unable to deal with, and still there was the fear that they might also be captured and made to suffer the same cruel death.

So the stranger was a welcome distraction, once he had allayed their fears that he was a spy. His knowledge of the scriptures, the intricate paths they took through the prophecies about Jesus, through the unfolding of God's eternal love for creation, turned their travelling from a chore to a joy. His words made many connections with things that Jesus had said, their minds were zipping back and forth, turning over new ways of understanding. The possibilities they raised, though barely comprehensible, if true, contained a hope, a fire that would be unquenchable.

Prayer

God of exodus,

who brought your people out of slavery,

into the abundance of the promised land,

we know that travelling is both necessary and risky

if we are to grow in life and faith.

We pray that you will guide our feet and minds

along the way of faith,

encouraging us to step beyond the borders of our fears

into your kingdom.

Amen.

Closing response

We praise you, O Lord, and we bless you:

**By your dying, death was destroyed,
by your rising, life was renewed,
by your Spirit, may we be filled with your glory.**

THE TENTH
STATION

Supper at
Emmaus

Le repas (Les bananes) – The Meal (The Bananas), **Paul Gauguin, 1891**

Familiarity and domesticity – customary food at a table that the disciples know well. Offering hospitality, allowing a stranger into their safe space, they find transformation exploding from the heart of their home.

Opening response

Jesus said: "I am the resurrection and the life."
Lord, you are our way, our truth and our life. Alleluia.

Reading

Luke 24:28-33

As they came near the village to which they were going, he walked ahead as if he were going on. But they urged him strongly, saying, "Stay with us, because it is almost evening and the day is now nearly over." So he went in to stay with them. When he was at the table with them, he took bread, blessed and broke it, and gave it to them. Then their eyes were opened, and they recognised him; and he vanished from their sight. They said to each other, "Were not our hearts burning within us while he was talking to us on the road, while he was opening the scriptures to us?" That same hour they got up and returned to Jerusalem; and they found the eleven and their companions gathered together.

Reflection

Was it just because they had reached the familiar territory of home, that the ground they walked on seemed greener, friendlier? Or had the stranger's opening up of the scriptures filled them with a fresh vision for life? Whichever, despite the rigours of the journey, their steps were lighter now than when they started. There was no hesitation about welcoming the stranger into their home, to meet their children. He was safe – well, not exactly safe, for his words had stirred something passionate in them – but certainly caring, not out to harm them. He was also obviously learned, a teacher, a holy man; it was only right that he was the one to lead prayers over the meal.

But then the unmistakable command: take, bless, break, share. It was not so much what he did, but the way he did it. The gestures were so familiar, the intonations in his voice so memorable, the stress on certain words that were worn into their consciousness. There was no other person this could possibly be. In his words on the road there had been the first glimmer of understanding, but in hospitality there was revelation. Christ is risen, he is risen indeed. And of course, in that moment he was gone, the lesson had been learned. It was a full night's journey back to Jerusalem, but they had just been fed by Jesus' own hand; they had a job to do and now they could delight in the strength to complete it.

Prayer

Lord Jesus Christ,

when you took bread and wine,

blessed them in the Father's name,

broke them open and shared them around the table,

you reached out to us

through the basic elements of food and drink.

As we remember your eternal sacrifice

through our celebration of the Eucharist,

may we share equally and fairly with the whole of your creation

all that sustains us and makes us whole.

Amen.

Closing response

We praise you, O Lord, and we bless you:
**By your dying, death was destroyed,
by your rising, life was renewed,
by your Spirit, may we be filled with your glory.**

THE ELEVENTH STATION

Jesus and Peter

Sheep Piece, **Henry Moore, 1971-1972**

Ewes and lambs know each other's distinctive bleats. As the mother calls her errant lamb home to suckle, so Christ calls Peter back to him. With forgiveness the Lamb of God offers a monumental, weighty calling – "Feed my lambs... tend my sheep... feed my sheep".

Opening response

Jesus said: "I am the resurrection and the life."
Lord, you are our way, our truth and our life. Alleluia.

Reading

John 21:15b-17. 19b

Jesus said to Simon Peter, "Simon son of John, do you love me more than these?" He said to him, "Yes, Lord; you know that I love you." Jesus said to him, "Feed my lambs." A second time he said to him, "Simon son of John, do you love me?" He said to him, "Yes, Lord; you know that I love you." Jesus said to him, "Tend my sheep." He said to him the third time, "Simon son of John, do you love me?" Peter felt hurt because he said to him the third time, "Do you love me?" And he said to him, "Lord, you know everything; you know that I love you." Jesus said to him, "Feed my sheep…" After this he said to him, "Follow me."

Reflection

Simon Peter was singled out for special treatment. Was this because he had been tasked with a special role – "You are the rock on which I will build my Church" – or because he had messed up in a spectacularly public way, denying his relationship with Jesus to anyone who spoke to him? Perhaps it was a bit of both. Notice Jesus' first question to him: "Simon son of John, do you love me more than these?" and Peter's careful reply: "Yes, Lord; you know that I love you." "You know that I love you." But not "more than these". Is this the first indication that something has changed in Simon Peter? Gone is the boastful alpha male of the Last Supper – "No, Lord, I'll not let you wash me… but not just my feet, but my head and my hands also", "No, Lord, everyone else might run away but I'll never, ever desert you."

There is enough reticence in that answer, enough self-knowledge, to assure Jesus that Simon Peter is ready for him to pursue his questioning. Jesus knows that this is going to hurt his friend, and he makes his interrogation very personal, each time calling him by name. But it has to be done. Simon Peter needs a way of being released from the guilt that has been haunting him over his cowardly actions, his outright denial of all he said he held dear. Guilt has broken his concentration, robbed him of his fisherman's skills; no longer can he read the signs in the water and weather that used to be second nature to him. He simply cannot get past what he has done.

One question, asked thrice; "Do you love me?" Each response an opportunity to wash away the guilt of denial. The reply "Feed my sheep" is an acknowledgement of trust being repaired and the final command, "Follow me", a renewal of Simon Peter's initial call. Like a ewe calling her wandering lamb, Jesus' repeated questions draw his faltering disciple home. The slate is wiped clean, Peter can start again. Perhaps, when Peter jumps out of the boat into the water to reach Jesus on the shore, that is the moment of his own baptism. Christ makes all things new.

Prayer

Holy God,

holy and strong,

holy and immortal,

have mercy on us.

We, like Peter, often stray,

we boast, or we dissemble, or we run from responsibility.

Speak to us, as you spoke to him,

so that we may know that we are forgiven,

and may strike out to share that forgiveness with all we meet.

Amen.

Closing response

We praise you, O Lord, and we bless you:

**By your dying, death was destroyed,
by your rising, life was renewed,
by your Spirit, may we be filled with your glory.**

THE TWELFTH STATION

Jesus Appears
to the Disciples

Christ Appearing to his Apostles after the Resurrection, **William Blake, c. 1795**

Are the disciples bowing down, awestruck, or awakening from torpor? Either way, there is no doubt whose presence they are in – pale from the grave, nevertheless a solid, muscular Christ who offers his wounded hands, a sign of his passion, to pull them out of despair into a post-Easter universe.

Opening response

Jesus said: "I am the resurrection and the life."
Lord, you are our way, our truth and our life. Alleluia.

Reading

Luke 24:36-43

While they were talking about this, Jesus himself stood among them and said to them, "Peace be with you." They were startled and terrified, and thought that they were seeing a ghost. He said to them, "Why are you frightened, and why do doubts arise in your hearts? Look at my hands and my feet; see that it is I myself. Touch me and see; for a ghost does not have flesh and bones as you see that I have." And when he had said this, he showed them his hands and his feet. While in their joy they were disbelieving and still wondering, he said to them, "Have you anything here to eat?" They gave him a piece of broiled fish, and he took it and ate in their presence.

Reflection

The physicality of the resurrection matters. Jesus alive as some form of spirit would not suffice or convince. The women need to take hold of him, to be reassured by the solidity of his presence, and for them it is his feet, which they have washed and cared for countless times, that enable them to grasp the truth of his resurrection – they know them, they are intimately familiar with their uniqueness. The men are more circumspect but they need the same reassurance, even if they don't like to admit it. That's why Jesus graciously gives them permission to examine his wounds. They look but don't touch. Disbelief still clouds their joy and they aren't completely convinced, so he asks for fish to eat. They watch as Jesus consumes the food; he is no ghost. This is not a collective hallucination. Jesus lives.

This knowledge – its depth and breadth – what are they going to do with it? Death is not the end; Jesus' prophecies about himself are vindicated. The kingdom of God that he preached about must be a reality. Again, what are they going to do about it? This isn't the end of fear and doubt, but it is the start of the ascendancy of a concrete, tangible hope. From now on, despite all the opposition and strife that will assail them, this miscellaneous band of followers are the agents of the peace with which Christ has blessed them, handing it on from generation to generation, from them to us, in the eager expectation that we will carry it forward, through the tough places and the receptive, building God's peaceable kingdom as we go.

Prayer

Christ, the Son of Righteousness,

the first resurrection gift you offered your disciples was "Peace be with you".

We pray that you will breathe your peace

over a world disfigured by conflict and disaster,

bringing comfort, rest and hope to all who are suffering,

and filling us with the faith, the vision, the compassion,

to go forth into the hard places as agents of your peace.

Amen.

Closing response

We praise you, O Lord, and we bless you:

**By your dying, death was destroyed,
by your rising, life was renewed,
by your Spirit, may we be filled with your glory.**

THE THIRTEENTH STATION

Thomas Meets his Lord

Doubting Thomas, **Duccio di Buoninsegna, 1308-1311**

Thomas looks intent and serious as he makes his approach to investigate Christ's proffered wounds. Everyone else holds back, but the top of the arch behind seems to link Christ and Thomas in this moment of intimacy. With his arm raised high, Christ looks about to offer his questioning, but perceptive, disciple a benediction.

Opening response

Jesus said: "I am the resurrection and the life."
Lord, you are our way, our truth and our life. Alleluia.

Reading

John 20:24-29

But Thomas (who was called the Twin), one of the twelve, was not with them when Jesus came. So the other disciples told him, "We have seen the Lord." But he said to them, "Unless I see the mark of the nails in his hands, and put my finger in the mark of the nails and my hand in his side, I will not believe."

A week later his disciples were again in the house, and Thomas was with them. Although the doors were shut, Jesus came and stood among them and said, "Peace be with you." Then he said to Thomas, "Put your finger here and see my hands. Reach out your hand and put it in my side. Do not doubt but believe." Thomas answered him, "My Lord and my God!" Jesus said to him, "Have you believed because you have seen me? Blessed are those who have not seen and yet have come to believe."

Reflection

All the disciples' need for certainty is focused now on one man – Thomas. It probably wasn't that he was the only one with doubts, nor was he the only one requiring that concrete, physical proof. He just happened to be the one out of the room at the time when Jesus first appeared. So his doubt provides a second opportunity for them all to be convinced. If his insistent fears can be laid to rest then perhaps they will all wholeheartedly believe.

Once again, Jesus offers the opportunity to reach out and touch his wounds. Scripture doesn't say whether Thomas actually puts his fingers in the scars, or his hand into the spear wound, but this is a direct command from Jesus and tradition has assumed from Jesus' words about believing "because you have seen me" that Thomas was the one to take this step.

Whatever occurs is enough to elicit Thomas' declaration: "My Lord and my God!" Whether he makes this response on behalf of the whole group or it is his own personal insight is not easy to tell. Certainly, the pool of believers who encounter Jesus after his resurrection is growing – first Mary Magdalene, then John and Peter, now Thomas. But each has much more to fathom, for revelation is only a beginning; how you make it live and breathe in your own being is what counts. Thomas not only took his new-found knowledge of the divinity of Jesus into his own heart, he carried it across continents into the heart of India. Christ was both the fuel for his journey and its goal. The truth he proclaimed lives with us still – whether we tell our neighbours, our nation or our enemies, it is a truth we cannot, must not, shall not, keep to ourselves.

Prayer

King of glory,

while we doubt, we fail, we turn away,

your faith in us remains strong.

May we experience that divine strength

coursing through our souls, bodies and minds,

so that our doubts may become the source of new knowledge,

leading us to see you more clearly,

and be drawn into the heart of your love for all creation.

Amen.

Closing response

We praise you, O Lord, and we bless you:

**By your dying, death was destroyed,
by your rising, life was renewed,
by your Spirit, may we be filled with your glory.**

THE FOURTEENTH
STATION

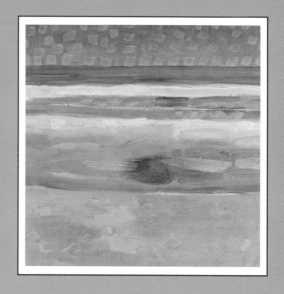

At the Sea
of Tiberias

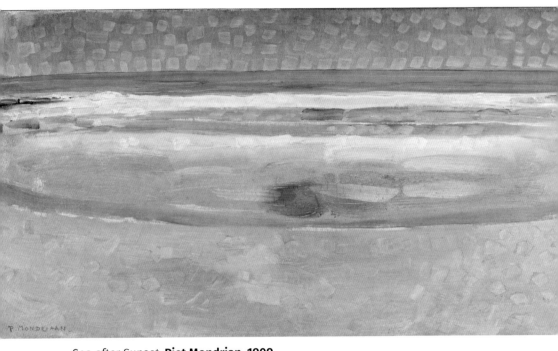

Sea after Sunset, **Piet Mondrian, 1909**

Sunset on the sea – will it be this calm in the morning? The harmony of colours presages a peaceful encounter; the horizon offers a hint of infinity. God is breaking through the boundaries of heaven to cook fish on the shore for his friends.

Opening response

Jesus said: "I am the resurrection and the life."
Lord, you are our way, our truth and our life. Alleluia.

Reading

John 21:1-6. 9-13

After these things Jesus showed himself again to the disciples by the Sea of Tiberias; and he showed himself in this way. Gathered there together were Simon Peter, Thomas called the Twin, Nathanael of Cana in Galilee, the sons of Zebedee, and two others of his disciples. Simon Peter said to them, "I am going fishing." They said to him, "We will go with you." They went out and got into the boat, but that night they caught nothing.

Just after daybreak, Jesus stood on the beach; but the disciples did not know that it was Jesus. Jesus said to them, "Children, you have no fish, have you?" They answered him, "No." He said to them, "Cast the net to the right side of the boat, and you will find some." So they cast it, and now they were not able to haul it in because there were so many fish…

When they had gone ashore, they saw a charcoal fire there, with fish on it, and bread. Jesus said to them, "Bring some of the fish that you have just caught." So Simon Peter went aboard and hauled the net ashore, full of large fish, a hundred and fifty-three of them; and though there were so many, the net was not torn. Jesus said to them, "Come and have breakfast." Now none of the disciples dared to ask him, "Who are you?" because they knew it was the Lord. Jesus came and took the bread and gave it to them, and did the same with the fish.

Reflection

Fish again, but this time it is Jesus offering food. As we heard, Simon Peter was trying to retrieve some sense of normality by doing what he knew best – fishing. But his preoccupations formed a growing web of confusion; both his concentration and his skills deserted him. The rest of the crew couldn't do any better.

Then a man on the shore offers instruction about catching fish. They could well be affronted: they are fishermen, the experts, not prone to taking advice from strangers. However, it has been a bad night and they are desperate for something positive to come out of their fruitless endeavours. So they cast the net on the other side and, lo and behold, it is full.

Back on the shore there is fish cooking, a fisherman's breakfast. With the catch they have just made there is plenty for all and no need to ask who this stranger is. Now they all know; the doubt has gone. Jesus is with them, alive, really alive. He is offering them food – a foretaste of the heavenly banquet perhaps? They can't have forgotten the feeding of enormous crowds four and five thousand strong. In his ministry Jesus gave spiritual and bodily nourishment; he came to his people incarnate as body, mind and spirit. This is the God of their familiar scriptures, the one who cares for the people, who feeds them in the desert and brings them out of adversity into the promised land. Jesus was by a lakeside when he called the disciples and asked them to become fishers of men; now he has got them fishing again. He's feeding them so they are ready to take on the next part of the journey.

Prayer

Lord Jesus, Bread of Life,

we give thanks to you,

for out of your compassion, out of your humanity,

you understood the needs of your disciples

and gave them both sustenance and hope.

We pray that all those who cry out to you in hunger

will be satisfied in body and spirit.

May all peoples be guided to share your riches,

and so be brought together to feast at one table

in your heavenly kingdom.

Amen.

Closing response

We praise you, O Lord, and we bless you:

By your dying, death was destroyed,
by your rising, life was renewed,
by your Spirit, may we be filled with your glory.

THE FIFTEENTH STATION

The Ascension

Cumulus Head, **Paul Nash, 1944**

Classical paintings of the ascension – a man rising in the air, clothes billowing, friends staring upwards awestruck – tend to be the least convincing, even ridiculous, images of Christ's story. Nash's *Cumulus Head* combines physicality with a monumental otherness, a transitory but telling sundering of the veil that divides earth from heaven.

Opening response

Jesus said: "I am the resurrection and the life."
Lord, you are our way, our truth and our life. Alleluia.

Reading

Mark 16:19-20

So then the Lord Jesus, after he had spoken to them, was taken up into heaven and sat down at the right hand of God. And they went out and proclaimed the good news everywhere, while the Lord worked with them and confirmed the message by the signs that accompanied it.

Reflection

The time is right. Certainly, the disciples will be bereft, another parting so soon after the last, but they are very different people now. The trauma of Jesus' death will never completely disappear – it will inform the way they treat others – but now it is laid out behind them through a resurrection lens. It has taken almost the whole of these fifty days to prepare the disciples for what is to come; where despair can turn to hope and doubt to belief. For the full impact of the crucifixion to be understood, for the divine reality of the resurrection to take hold, they had to experience the complexities of these holy mysteries little by little, in human time; there couldn't have been a smooth, simple transition. Now they are ready. Jesus has to leave, to let them get on with forming his body here on earth.

Granted, they gaze up into space for a while after he's gone and, according to Luke, need prompting from a couple of angels to get them grounded again; but then they apply themselves. There is a divine message to be told and they are the messengers. How they are going to accomplish their mission will take some sorting out: each disciple is blessed with their own skills and resources, each has been touched by Jesus in their own unique way and has their own particular view of what actually happened. Each reacted to Jesus' ascension differently. Mark tells us that they are quick to go out into the streets and villages – "immediately" he says. Matthew implicitly agrees, underscoring their course of action with the famous four commands: "Go, make disciples, baptise and teach." Luke gives the disciples credit for having learned from Jesus the importance of prayer before action and tracks their journey back to Jerusalem to spend time together before hitting the road. However they react, the ascension will release the disciples to use their knowledge, experience, faith and wills to begin building the kingdom of God here on earth.

Prayer

Eternal God,

through your birth and death, resurrection and ascension,

you split open the veil that hides heaven from earth.

In baptism you reach out your hand,

to draw us home into your gracious presence.

Emboldened by your Spirit may we proclaim the good news with

faithful passion,

encouraging others to break through their own fears

into the never-ending embrace of your love.

Amen.

Closing response

We praise you, O Lord, and we bless you:

**By your dying, death was destroyed,
by your rising, life was renewed,
by your Spirit, may we be filled with your glory.**

THE SIXTEENTH STATION

Pentecost

Blue and Green Music, **Georgia O'Keeffe, 1921**

We start with the constrictions of the tomb; we end with the disciples walled up in a room, doors and windows bolted, in the dark of their self-made grave. Even so, the Spirit breaks through, affirming and releasing them into new life. *Blue and Green Music* plays with the colours of earth and water, of nurturing, of the elements required for germination. Barriers are broken and tiny shoots of fresh life emerge, each with a different line to write in the next chapter of the story of God and creation.

Opening response

Jesus said: "I am the resurrection and the life."

Lord, you are our way, our truth and our life. Alleluia.

Reading

Acts 2:1-4

When the day of Pentecost had come, they were all together in one place. And suddenly from heaven there came a sound like the rush of a violent wind, and it filled the entire house where they were sitting. Divided tongues, as of fire, appeared among them, and a tongue rested on each of them. All of them were filled with the Holy Spirit and began to speak in other languages, as the Spirit gave them ability.

Reflection

The resurrection appearances may be over, but with the irruption of the Spirit, God's eternal and intimate relationship with creation continues. One Spirit, divided like flames, or gusts of wind, inspires the individuals in the room, each to their own ability. So Peter develops his latent preaching skills, some of the followers find their gifts as healers, still others discover that their organisational abilities are sharpened up. Certainly, for all of them, there is a greater attendance on the word of God – whether expressed through scripture, their memories of Jesus, or their interaction with the world.

They will leave the room, their safe space, to travel into the city and beyond, carrying out those final commands of Jesus. The Church is born and now they have only to pinch their own flesh to know what the body of Christ feels like.

The resurrection began with a great boulder of limestone sealing Jesus' body into the tomb. To all intents and purposes, it was a full stop, the end of the story. But with God there is no final full stop, only an ellipsis; there is no end, for the journey continues and we have only to pinch our own flesh to know what the body of Christ feels like today. The commands are still the same – "Go, make disciples, baptise and teach" – yet the promise too remains as fresh as it was to that first band of followers: Christ will be with us, even until the end of time.

Prayer

Living Lord,

risen, ascended, returning, through this way of light,

you have reminded us that darkness is part of the journey.

You have shared with us the revelation of your glory.

You have challenged us to be the next chapter in your resurrection story.

Send forth your Holy Spirit upon us,

that we might kindle and tend the fires of your love

throughout all creation.

Amen.

Closing response

We praise you, O Lord, and we bless you:

**By your dying, death was destroyed,
by your rising, life was renewed,
by your Spirit may we be filled with your glory.**

Prayers at the end of the service

Concluding responses, prayers and blessing

We pray together for the flourishing of God's kingdom in the words Jesus himself taught us:

Our Father in heaven,

hallowed be your name,

your kingdom come,

your will be done,

on earth as in heaven.

Give us today our daily bread.

Forgive us our sins

as we forgive those who sin against us.

Lead us not into temptation

but deliver us from evil.

For the kingdom, the power,

and the glory are yours

now and for ever.

Amen.

Almighty God,

through your risen Son, Jesus Christ,

you broke the tyranny of sin and death

to raise us up in the way of truth.

With our hearts and minds set on him,

and empowered by the Holy Spirit,

may we continually work

to build your kingdom

to your praise and glory.

Amen.

Alleluia. Christ is risen.
He is risen indeed. Alleluia.

Christ has offered us each a place at his holy table.
**He has called us to take and bless, break and share,
he has called us to welcome everyone to his feast.**

Alleluia. Christ is risen.
He is risen indeed. Alleluia.

Christ has claimed us to be his body in the world.
**He charged us to be his hands, his feet,
to be his compassionate eyes, to offer his blessing.**

Alleluia. Christ is risen.
He is risen indeed. Alleluia.

Holy God,

holy and strong,

holy and immortal,

by whose glory Christ burst forth from the tomb,

a seed laid to rest in darkness

but blossoming as the one true light:

may all who have walked this resurrection way

be faithful witnesses to his risen life;

and the blessing of God almighty,

the Father, the Son, and the Holy Spirit,

be among you and remain with you always.

Amen.

Producing your own stations

Pictorial representations are an important component of this devotional journey. However, not everyone will have access to a relevant set of illustrations and may prefer alternative visual images.

This section offers some suggestions for a physical set of stations - a sequential gathering of symbolic "props" to enrich the meditations - which with considerable flexibility can be adapted to time, place and objects at hand. The intention for each station is to enable participants to focus upon the main elements explored in the biblical text and reflections, and to stimulate the imagination by making use of the church or worship space in your own creative ways.

THE FIRST STATION: The Sealed Tomb

Gather in front of a closed door, perhaps locked with the key visible. This is likely to be in the porch, or normal entrance into church. If the door has transparent or glass sections, ensure that all lights are off inside (except, if you have one, a sanctuary lamp and the Paschal candle). Begin the service here with the opening prayers and first meditation. At the end of the station, unlock the door and walk through it to the second station.

THE SECOND STATION: The Resurrection

Present a cardboard box, lined on the inside with gold or silver paper, resting on its side with the flaps just open, facing the people; inside, a small gold- or silver-covered pot containing a seedling. To soften the harshness of the box you may wish to surround it with swathes of material in gold, green or spring colours of new life.

THE THIRD STATION: They Found the Stone Rolled Away

Either: If you have a stone font in a suitable position, then remove the cover and give everyone the opportunity to view its emptiness and feel the cold, hard, strength of the stone.

Or: Place large stones securely on a plinth, table or chair covered with a cloth; invite participants to touch the stones.

THE FOURTH STATION: The Women at the Tomb

An assemblage of scattered aromatic herbs and spices on a table, an unlabelled glass bottle of oil and an additional bottle containing coloured water to represent perfume for anointing.

THE FIFTH STATION: The Women Meet the Risen Lord

A pair of painted footprints (using poster paint or similar), revealing the lines and marks of the feet, surrounded by a ring of white (for resurrection) and red (for the scars on the feet) flowers or petals, arranged on the floor.

THE SIXTH STATION: Peter and John Run to the Tomb

Display prominently two contrasting pairs of men's shoes: for example, battered work boots and neat formal shoes; wellington boots and running shoes or trainers.

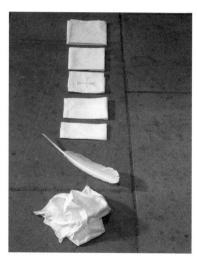

THE SEVENTH STATION: Angels at the Empty Tomb

Preferably on a stone floor, present a row of neatly folded white cloths or fair linen separated by a large white feather from a crumpled-up white handkerchief.

THE EIGHTH STATION: Mary Magdalene Meets the Risen Lord

An assemblage of horticultural equipment – a watering can, trowel, garden fork or spade – alongside a few small pots of growing plants.

THE NINTH STATION: The Walk to Emmaus

Against a suitable pillar or plinth, display a selection of walking gear - a rucksack and walking pole, for example - interwoven with brambles (take care when handling these).

THE TENTH STATION: Supper at Emmaus

You may have an altar that can be used appropriately to present broken bread on a tray and a cup of wine; otherwise a small table with these elements, or a table laid with three place settings.

THE ELEVENTH STATION: Jesus and Peter

Pictures of different sheep breeds in contrasting settings; any shepherding accoutrements that may be available - sheep shears, a shepherd's crook (which could be cut from cardboard or fashioned from a straight branch), a small amount of fleece or fibre.

THE TWELFTH STATION: Jesus Appears to the Disciples

Arranged on a table, several anatomical drawings or open book(s) with illustrations of the human body; a small artist's manikin; a padlock.

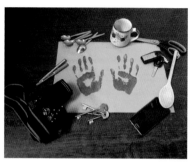

THE THIRTEENTH STATION: Thomas Meets his Lord

Create a pair of painted handprints (using poster paint - see the fifth station) and display them on a table, surrounded by a circle of objects we might handle every day – pens, keys, a mobile phone, cutlery, etc.

THE FOURTEENTH STATION: At the Sea of Tiberias

A fishing net, shells, some kindling and matches arranged on the floor (decorative nets can be obtained easily and cheaply online).

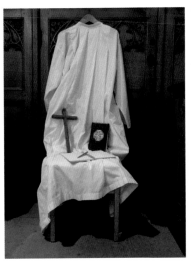

THE FIFTEENTH STATION: The Ascension

Place a plain cross, a Bible and a blank notebook on the bottom section of a white alb or surplice draped over a chair; the top half of the garment should be hung against a suitable background.

THE SIXTEENTH STATION: Pentecost

Return to the original doorway, this time from the inside, with votive candles and the Paschal candle nearby. After lighting the votive candles from the Paschal candle and giving one to each person, open the door and continue with the reflection. At the end of the station invite everyone back into the porch, looking out to the world for the final prayers.

Music for the journey

Just as singing while walking between each station has long been an integral aspect of the Stations of the Cross, musical accompaniment is set to become an established tradition for the Stations of the Resurrection. While many glorious Easter hymns and songs exist, however, few so far are replete with a sufficient number of verses to accommodate sixteen or more stations. Those that I have suggested were chosen partly for their numerous, short verses, but also because they resound with joyful alleluias. Repeating verses of a single hymn or combining hymns to extend to the full length of the service can work equally effectively.

My particular favourite, "Christ is the King, O friends rejoice!", has a short verse form and a lively melody; so offered here is a new "processional" – a set of words to the same Vulpius tune, *Gelobt Sei Gott*, providing a simple narrative to begin after the opening prayers and thereafter accompany movement between each station. In addition there is a concluding verse for the transition to the final prayers and blessing.

Alternatively, Taizé chant feels especially suited to this form of devotion and I have suggested a small selection below. On a practical level, the need for lengthy material to be reproduced in a participants' booklet is obviated if a single refrain is chosen; but, more importantly, these simple, repetitive chants can serve to reinforce the rhythm of prayer and song that is inherent in the Stations of the Resurrection, holding our devotions together as an onward pilgrim journey.

Hymns

Christ the Lord is risen again!
Tune: *Orientis Partibus* or *Württemberg*

Jesus lives! thy terrors now
Tune: *St Albinus*

Christ is the King, O friends rejoice!
Tune: Vulpius *(Gelobt Sei Gott)*

Alleluia, Alleluia, give thanks to the risen Lord
Tune: Alleluia No. 199 and refrain

Ye sons and daughters of the King
Tune: *O Filii et Filiae*

Chants

Laudate Dominum	Taizé, refrain only
Surrexit Dominus vere	Taizé
Bless the Lord, my soul	Taizé, refrain only

Processional

(Tune: Vulpius – *Gelobt Sei Gott*)

1. Cold is the tomb in dead of night,
    Easter arising out of sight,
    quickened by ray of morning light.
    Alleluia, alleluia, alleluia.

2. Deep in the soil lies buried grain,
    from shadows dark bursts life again,
    hope now set free sings love's refrain:
    Alleluia…

3. Entrance unguarded, stone rolled free,
    death broken open, Christ the key,
    to live as God would have us be.
    Alleluia…

4. Anointing oil, still showing care,
    empty the tomb, cries of despair;
    angels reply, "He is not there!"
    Alleluia…

5. Growing in faith fresh as the dew,
    see their belov'd and round him drew,
    cradling his feet, weeping anew.
    Alleluia…

6. Peter and John, both with one thought,
    run to the tomb breathlessly wrought:
    is Christ alive just as he taught?
    Alleluia…

7. Mary, grieving, is garden bound,
   his body gone, her hope is drowned,
   weeping she cries: "Will he be found?"
   Alleluia…

8. Weeping she cries, cast down by shame,
   "Mary!" she hears, he calls her name;
   "I am your Lord: my life proclaim."
   Alleluia…

9. Emmaus their goal, walking by day,
   stranger comes by – what does he say?
   Scriptures explored, learning the Way.
   Alleluia…

10. "Night has come down, stay is our prayer."
    He raises bread to bless, break, share.
    Hearts burn within; Jesus was there.
    Alleluia…

11. Christ on the shore, Peter at sea,
    "Tend all my lambs, feed them for me."
    Peter has learnt – love sets him free.
    Alleluia…

12. Doors bolted tightly, locked in fear;
    yet in their midst Christ does appear:
    "Peace be with you", the Lord is here.
    Alleluia…

13. Thomas the twin must touch the pain,
    Christ bares his wounds his soul to gain:
    "My Lord and God, within me reign."
    Alleluia…

14. No fish that night, a fire ashore:
    "Cast out your nets, you will catch more!"
    He fed them then, their glad hearts soar.
    Alleluia…

15. On holy hill they see him rise,
    taken to God before their eyes.
    Their work begins; grace is the prize.
    Alleluia…

16. The Church is born, sent out to preach,
    following Christ, his love to teach,
    spiritual fire, inspiring each.
    Alleluia…

17. Christ is alive, so let us sing
    glorious praise to God our king!
    Out to the world this news we bring:
    Alleluia…

Picture acknowledgements: Front cover and pp 31, 32: Lorenzo Monaco [Public domain], from Wikimedia Commons; p 8: The Flax Bourton Swallowtail, Richard Greatrex, acrylic and gold leaf on wood, 2015. pp13,14: sculpture: en:Ben Nicholson (d 1982); photo: Wmpearl [CC0], from Wikimedia Commons; pp 19,20 Georgia O'Keeffe [Public domain], via Wikimedia Commons; pp 25,26: Ross Irving on behalf of the Barns-Graham Trust [CC BY-SA 4.0 (https://creativecommons. org/licenses/by-sa/4.0)], from Wikimedia Commons; pp 37,38: Paul Gauguin [Public domain]; pp 43,44: Kamahele [CC BY-SA 3.0 (https:// creativecommons.org/licenses/by-sa/3.0)], from Wikimedia Commons; pp 49,50: James Tissot [Public domain]; pp 55,56: Samuel Palmer [Public domain]; pp 61,62: Paul Nash [Public domain]; pp 67,68: Paul Gauguin [Public domain]; pp 73,74: © Roland Fischer, Zürich (Switzerland) – Mail notification to: roland_zh(at)hispeed(dot)ch / Wikimedia Commons; pp 78,80: William Blake [Public domain]; pp 85,86: Duccio di Buoninsegna [Public domain]; pp 91,92: Piet Mondrian [Public domain]; pp 97,98: Paul Nash [Public domain], via Wikimedia Commons; pp 103,104: Georgia O'Keeffe [Public domain]; pp 113-118: © Richard Q. Greatrex.

Every effort has been made to trace copyright holders and to obtain their permission for the use of copyright material. The publisher apologises for any errors or omissions and would be grateful for notification of any corrections that should be incorporated in future reprints or editions of this book.

Richard Greatrex is a parish priest and bookseller with a particular interest in liturgy and the arts. He encourages others to deepen their spirituality through engagement with music, poetry, literature and the visual arts, often using aspects of secular culture to illuminate elements of faith. The genesis of this book was a growing longing to counteract the diminishing of Eastertide in Church and beyond from a lengthy season to a single day, and a desire to restore the joy, wonder, celebrations, challenges and hope of the Great Fifty Days of Easter.